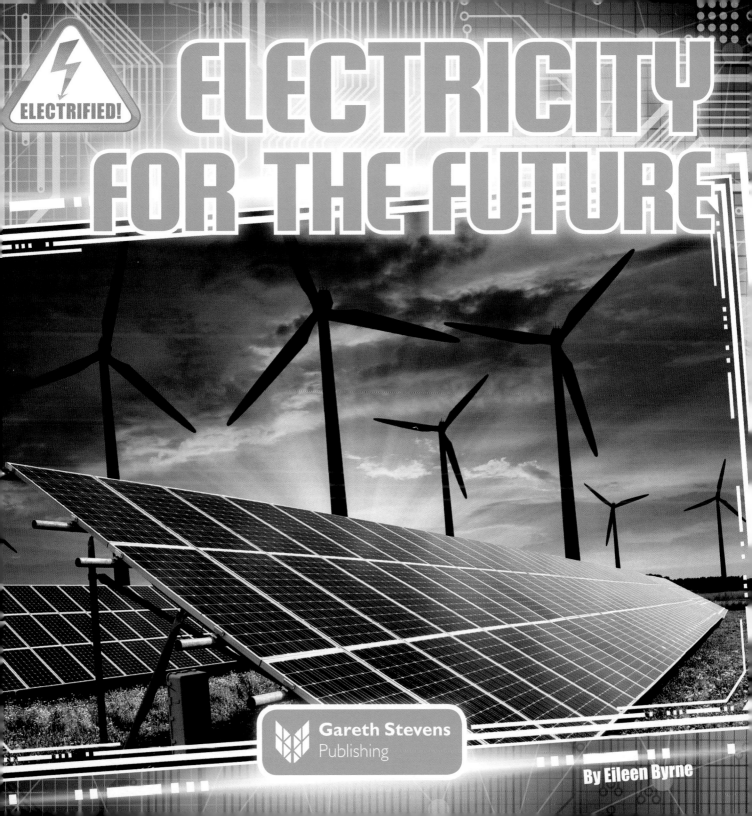

ELECTRIFIED!

ELECTRICITY FOR THE FUTURE

Gareth Stevens Publishing

By Eileen Byrne

Please visit our website, www.garethstevens.com. For a free color catalog of all our high-quality books, call toll free 1-800-542-2595 or fax 1-877-542-2596.

Library of Congress Cataloging-in-Publication Data

Byrne, Eileen, 1978- author.
Electricity for the future / Eileen Byrne.
    pages cm. — (Electrified!)
Includes index.
ISBN 978-1-4339-8395-5 (paperback)
ISBN 978-1-4339-8396-2 (6-pack)
ISBN 978-1-4339-8394-8 (library binding)
1. Electric power—Juvenile literature. 2. Electricity—Juvenile literature. I. Title.
TK1001.B97 2013
333.793'2—dc23

2012020374

First Edition

Published in 2013 by
Gareth Stevens Publishing
111 East 14th Street, Suite 349
New York, NY 10003

Copyright © 2013 Gareth Stevens Publishing

Designer: Katelyn E. Reynolds
Editor: Therese Shea

Photo credits: Cover, p. 1 Vaclav Volrab/Shutterstock.com; cover, pp. 1 (logo), 15, 17, 19 iStockphoto/Thinkstock.com; cover, pp. 1, 3–24 (background) Lukas Radavicius/Shutterstock.com; cover, pp. 1, 3–24 (image frame) VikaSuh/Shutterstock.com; p. 5 Brand X Pictures/Thinkstock.com; p. 7 Photodisc/Thinkstock.com; pp. 9, 11 Hemera/Thinkstock.com; p. 13 Susan Thompson Photography/Getty Images; p. 21 © iStockphoto.com/Sjo.

Printed in the United States of America

CPSIA compliance information: Batch #CW13GS: For further information contact Gareth Stevens, New York, New York at 1-800-542-2595.

CONTENTS

Our Electric World 4

Batteries and Generators 6

Fossil Fuels 8

Water Energy 10

Wind Energy 12

Solar Energy 14

Geothermal Energy 16

Biomass Energy 18

Hydrogen and the Future 20

Glossary 22

For More Information 23

Index 24

Words in the glossary appear in **bold** type the first time they are used in the text.

OUR ELECTRIC WORLD

Electricity runs through all matter on Earth—even through you and me! Beginning in the 1800s, scientists found ways to control electrical power. Now we use this power, or energy, for countless things that make our lives easier and more fun. From lighting a dark room to texting a friend, electricity makes it happen.

Electricity isn't created. It's **converted** from other kinds of energy. Some ways that we get electrical energy have a harmful effect on Earth. In the future, we may need to adopt new ways of getting electricity.

POWER FACT!

Electricity and magnetism make up a force called electromagnetism. This force holds together the **particles** that are the building blocks of every bit of matter in the universe!

4

Can you imagine how different your life would be without electricity?

5

BATTERIES AND GENERATORS

Devices such as batteries and generators convert energy into electrical power. A battery converts **chemical** energy into a flow of electrical energy. However, the chemical energy runs out. This is why your cell phone or battery-powered calculator needs new batteries after a time. Rechargeable batteries can be refueled by more electricity. Other batteries just become trash.

Generators convert **mechanical** energy into electrical energy. Even the simplest generator requires a metal coil and a magnet. The movement of one near the other causes an electric **current**.

POWER FACT!

A generator only works if the metal coil is made of a conductor. A conductor is matter through which **electrons** flow easily, such as copper. This flow of electrons is the current.

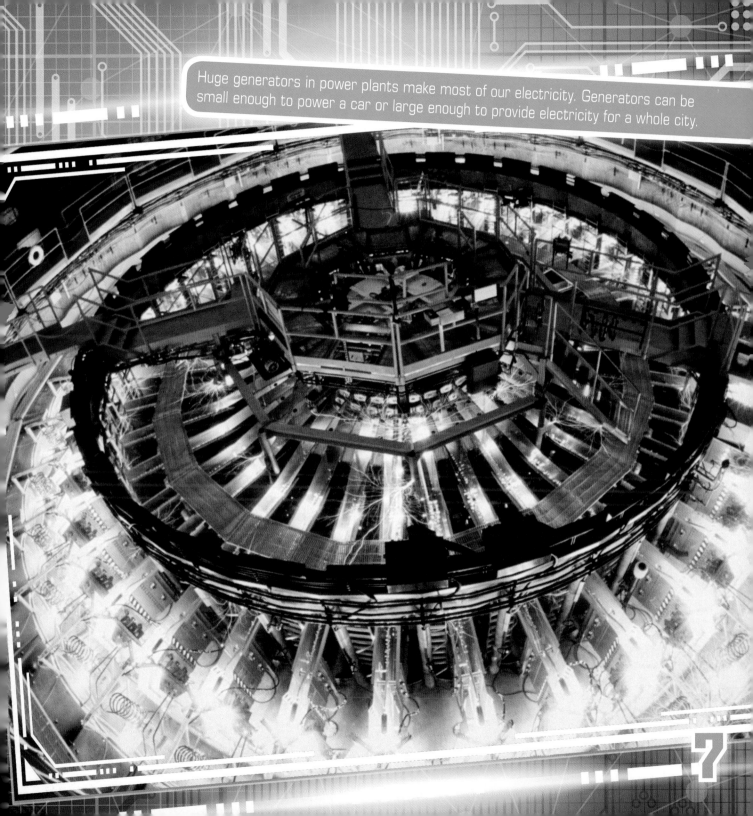

Huge generators in power plants make most of our electricity. Generators can be small enough to power a car or large enough to provide electricity for a whole city.

7

FOSSIL FUELS

Different sources provide the movement, or the mechanical energy, needed to run generators. Coal, natural gas, and oil are burned to create heat or steam, which moves parts of the generator to produce an electric current.

These "fossil fuels" formed over millions of years from plant and animal remains. They're called nonrenewable resources because they can't be replaced easily. Another problem with fossil fuels is their contribution to **climate change**. Also, as they're burned, they give off gases and particles that are harmful to people's health.

POWER FACT!

Nuclear power uses **fission** to heat water into steam to power a generator. It creates a lot of electricity, but its waste is very dangerous.

About 68 percent of the electricity created in the United States comes from fossil fuels.

9

WATER ENERGY

The dangers of fossil fuels and nuclear power have made people look for cleaner, more renewable sources of energy. Water is one plentiful renewable resource. The mechanical energy provided by a gushing waterfall or rushing river can easily power a generator. This is called hydroelectricity.

Water is the most used renewable energy resource. Though it produces less waste than fossil fuels, it still has drawbacks. Hydroelectricity is currently a more costly process than fossil fuel electricity. Dams affect communities of people, animals, and plants.

POWER FACT!

Hydroelectricity powers about 7 percent of the United States and about 19 percent of the world.

Water rushing through this dam provides the mechanical energy needed to power a generator. In some places, hydroelectricity depends on rainfall and climate.

11

WIND ENERGY

Wind spins the blades on a **turbine** and converts mechanical energy into electrical power. Often many turbines are grouped into one space called a wind farm. These can produce a great amount of electricity.

While wind turbines don't give off harmful pollution, there are some disadvantages. Many people don't want to live near them. In addition, in order for a wind turbine to work well, wind speeds usually must be above 12 miles (19 km) per hour. If winds are too strong, the turbines must be turned off.

POWER FACT!

California has enough wind to produce 11 percent of the world's wind electricity.

Some farmers have welcomed turbines onto their land. Their cattle wander around the turbines freely.

SOLAR ENERGY

Another plentiful renewable energy resource for creating electricity is sunlight. Heat energy from the sun is used to produce steam to power generators. It can also be used to charge devices called solar cells. These directly convert solar energy into electricity without the need for generators.

Solar energy is clean energy, and cells placed on buildings don't take up too much room. However, solar cells are costly. And if the sun doesn't shine brightly every day, batteries are needed to produce power.

Solar cells need a lot of surface area to collect enough energy to be useful.

GEOTHERMAL ENERGY

Yet another renewable energy resource isn't on Earth, it's in it! Earth's center, or core, is extremely hot. This heat escapes to the surface in certain places, such as volcanoes and **hot springs**.

Power plants can use the hot water and steam found in geothermal **reservoirs** to produce electricity. Some reservoirs are found close to the surface. However, sometimes people drill down a mile or more to find a heat source. Once they do, they can use the heat energy to power generators.

POWER FACT!

Most of the geothermal reservoirs in the United States are located in the West and Hawaii.

Like other renewable resources, geothermal energy has drawbacks. Geothermal reservoirs aren't found everywhere, and it's possible for them to "dry up."

17

BIOMASS ENERGY

Biomass fuel sounds fancy, but it isn't new. People have burned wood for heat for thousands of years. Certain power plants burn biomass waste and other trash to run generators. One positive part of waste-to-energy power plants is that less waste goes to landfills. However, a disadvantage is that burning chemical waste can let dangerous particles escape into the air.

Rotting waste in landfills creates the gases methane and carbon dioxide, both contributors to climate change. However, some power plants burn these to generate electricity. This could help slow climate change!

HYDROGEN AND THE FUTURE

Hydrogen is the most plentiful element on Earth. Hydrogen fuel cells are devices that change hydrogen to electricity using chemical energy. They give off no pollution and actually make water! As a fuel, hydrogen is powerful enough to launch rockets into space! However, it's only found attached to other elements and must be separated first.

Scientists will continue to look for ways to make hydrogen and other renewable resources less costly and more accepted alternatives to fossil fuels. How do you think electricity will be produced in the future?

ALTERNATIVES TO FOSSIL FUEL ENERGY

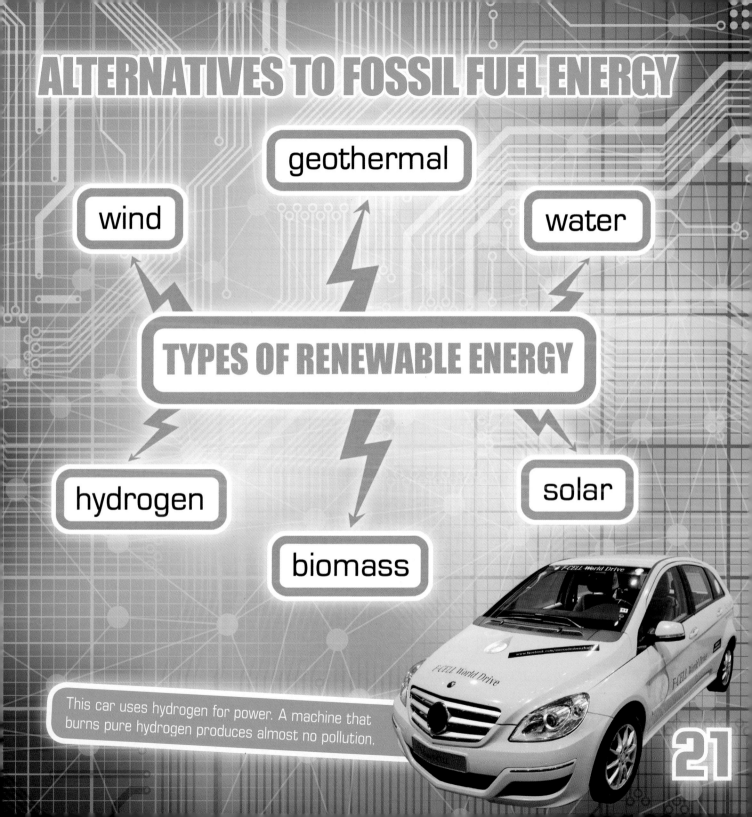

geothermal

wind

water

TYPES OF RENEWABLE ENERGY

hydrogen

solar

biomass

This car uses hydrogen for power. A machine that burns pure hydrogen produces almost no pollution.

21

GLOSSARY

biomass: plant matter and animal waste used to produce energy

chemical: relating to the use of chemicals, or matter that can be mixed with other matter to cause changes

climate change: long-term change in weather, resulting partly from human activity

convert: to cause to change form

current: a flow of electricity resulting from the movement of particles such as electrons

device: a tool or machine made to perform a task

electron: a particle found in atoms that acts as a carrier of electricity in solids

fission: the dividing or splitting of the nucleus, or center, of an atom to release energy

hot spring: a source of water heated by warmth from inside Earth

hydrogen: a colorless, odorless gas that is the most common element on Earth

mechanical: relating to physical movement

particle: a very small piece of something

reservoir: a place where something is stored

turbine: a motor operated by the movement of water, steam, or air

FOR MORE INFORMATION

Books

Orme, Helen. *Energy for the Future*. New York, NY: Bearport Publishing, 2008.

Oxlade, Chris. *Energy: Present Knowledge, Future Trends*. North Mankato, MN: Smart Apple Media, 2004.

Walker, Sally M. *Investigating Electricity*. Minneapolis, MN: Lerner Publications, 2012.

Websites

EIA Energy Kids—Renewable
www.eia.gov/kids/energy.cfm?page=renewable_home-basics
Learn more about renewable energy resources and find links to other energy topics.

Energy Story
energyquest.ca.gov/story/
Read about the many ways people harness the power of nature to make electricity.

INDEX

batteries 6, 14

biomass fuel 18, 21

carbon dioxide 18

chemical energy 6, 20

clean energy 10, 14

climate change 8, 18

coal 8

conductor 6

current 6, 8

electromagnetism 4

electrons 6

fossil fuels 8, 9, 10, 20, 21

generators 6, 7, 8, 10, 11, 14, 16, 18

geothermal energy 16, 17, 21

geothermal reservoirs 16, 17

hydroelectricity 10, 11

hydrogen 20, 21

mechanical energy 6, 8, 10, 11, 12

methane 18

natural gas 8

nonrenewable resources 8

nuclear power 8, 10

oil 8

particles 4, 8, 18

pollution 12, 20, 21

power plants 7, 16, 18

renewable resources 10, 14, 16, 17, 20, 21

solar cells 14, 15

solar energy 14, 21

steam 8, 14, 16

turbines 12, 13

water 8, 10, 11, 16, 20, 21

wind 12, 21

wind farm 12